# God's Heart on
# MORMONISM
## A Different gospel
## A Different god

BY JUNE HUNT

HOPE
*for the Heart*

P.O. Box 7 • Dallas, Texas • 75221

## *Also by June Hunt*

### God's Heart On Mini-Books

- Atheism & Agnosticism
- Childhood Sexual Abuse
- Cults
- Decision Making
- Guilt
- Holy Spirit

- Mormonism
- Occult, The
- Parenting
- Spiritual Warfare
- Victimization

### Hope Mini-Books

- *Hope & Help for Sexual Addiction*
- *Hope & Healing from Wife Abuse*

### Books

*Bonding with Your Teen Through Boundaries*

*Healing the Hurting Heart*

*Seeing Yourself Through God's Eyes*

Scripture taken from the HOLY BIBLE, NEW INTERNATIONAL VERSION. NIV. Copyright 1973, 1978, 1984 by International Bible Society. Used by permission of Zondervan Publishing House. All rights reserved.

ISBN: 1-931734-00-3

To order the *Heart of the Matter Series* or other material related to Mormonism, write HOPE FOR THE HEART • P.O. Box 7 • Dallas, TX • 75221 or call toll-free **1-800-488-HOPE (4673).**
**www.hopefortheheart.org**

# *Preface*

Have you ever thought you were so right, then realized you were so wrong? Have you ever assumed something was clearly true, yet later found it was completely false? Truthfully, I know what it's like to be sincere . . . and sincerely wrong! And so does James Walker.

James and I both care about people who are "sincerely wrong." We deeply care that people traveling the wrong direction not just turn around, but also turn onto the right road and travel in the way God would have them to go.

I've chosen to share James Walker's testimony with you because of his background. I personally know James to be sincere, earnest and trustworthy. And I pray that as you read his testimony and the following pages about Mormonism, the Lord will open your eyes so that you will see truth in its fullness.

The truth you learn about the Latter-day Saints could keep you—or someone you love—from being "sincere, yet sincerely wrong."

—June Hunt

# I Bear You My Testimony*

*By James Walker*

As a member of the Church of Jesus Christ of Latter-day Saints, I believed that Joseph Smith was a true prophet of God and that the LDS Church was the only true church on earth. You see, I was born into an LDS home. My father's side of the family had been members of the Church for four generations. At the age of eight I was baptized into the LDS church and received the laying on of hands for the gift of the Holy Ghost.

From that early age to adulthood, I was involved in many aspects of Mormon life. I tithed and attended Priesthood, fast and testimony, and Sacrament meetings. I also performed my duty in our Family Home Evening and Home Teaching. I even obtained my temple recommend and entered the Salt Lake City temple to perform baptism for the dead.

As my commitment increased, a good friend of mine, who was not a member of the Church, became concerned about me. He had been researching the LDS church and shared some facts I didn't know. I began to wonder about my personal salvation. Although I was in good standing with the Church, I was not sure I was keeping all the laws. I also read in the book of Mormon, *". . . it is by grace that we are saved, after all we can do."*[1]

The god I worshiped as a Latter-day Saint was very different from the God of the Bible. I had worshiped *"God the Eternal Father, His Son Jesus Christ, and the Holy Ghost."*[2] The names were right—but the god was wrong.

The god that I worshiped as a Latter-day Saint had a body of flesh and bone,[3] was a glorified, exalted man,[4] and was one of many gods.[5]

I even learned that the Mormon god has Eternal Wives through whom spirit children are born[6] and these children have the potential to become other gods.[7] However, the God of the Bible does not have a body of flesh and bone. *"God is a Spirit . . . ; A spirit hath not flesh and bones."* He is not a man who was exalted to godhood. *"God is not a man. . . ."*[8] The God of the Bible has no wife and stands alone as God.[9]

I followed what Mormonism taught me about getting to heaven. Its gospel—its message about how to get to heaven—included *"all of the laws, principles, rites, ordinances, acts, powers, authorities, and keys necessary to save and exalt men in the highest heaven hereafter."*[10] So Mormonism's full salvation comes through a combination of faith, baptism in the church, and works.[11]

The Bible's Gospel message focuses on Christ. When He died for us on the cross, we were forgiven and offered eternal life. To avoid any confusion, the Bible clearly explains that the Gospel does not include laws, or ordinances, or works.[12]

*Mormonism and the Bible teach two different messages about getting to heaven. In fact, they are direct opposites. Both can't be true; I had to choose one or the other.*

As a Mormon, I thought I had been trusting Christ as my personal Savior, but I was really trusting my testimony and my good works for salvation. I finally knelt down and admitted to my Heavenly Father that even on my best days I was not perfect. I, like everyone else, was a sinner.[13] It was hard, but I told God I was no longer going to trust in my own good works or any church for eternal life. From that time on, I was going to trust His Son Jesus Christ alone to save me from my sins.[14, 15]

I urge you to come to the God of the Bible, the only true God.[16] He loves you and sent His Son Jesus Christ to die for your sins.[17] You can find wonderful freedom when you admit to God that you are a sinner and trust Christ alone as your Savior.[18]

> *"And this is the testimony:*
> *God has given us eternal life,*
> *and this life is in His Son*
> *He who has the Son has life;*
> *he who does not have the*
> *Son of God does not have life."*
> *(1 John 5:11-12)*

\* Adapted from *I Bear You My Testimony* @ American Tract Society (1-800-54-TRACT). Used by permission.

1  2 Nephi 25:23.

2  First Article of Faith; McConkie, Mormon Doctrine (MD), 1966, p. 270.

3  Doctrine and Covenants (D &C) 130:22

4  Gospel Through the Ages (GTA), 1945, p. 104.

5  MD, pp. 576-577.

6  Ibid., p. 516;

7  Ibid., p. 745, Achieving a Celestial Marriage, 1976, p. 132.

8  John 4:24; Luke 24:39; Numbers 23:19; Psalm 90:2.

9  Isaiah 43:10; 44:6; 46:9.

10  MD, p. 331.

11  Ibid., pp. 669-70; Ensign, Nov. 1982, p. 61; Moroni 10:32-33; 3 Nephi 27:19; Alma 12:16-18; 34:32-35.

12  1 Corinthians 15:1-8; Acts 10:43; John 3:16; Romans 3:19-24; Colossians 2:16-17; Titus 3:5-7.

13  Romans 3:23.

14  Acts 4:12.

15  Ephesians 2:8-9.

16  Deuteronomy 4:35, 39.

17  John 3:16.

18  Isaiah 53:6; Acts 13:39; Romans 10:9-13.

# GOD'S HEART ON MORMONISM
## A DIFFERENT GOSPEL— A DIFFERENT GOD

## I. DEFINITIONS ............................ 11-25

Where did the Name *Mormon* Come From?
Who are the *Latter-day Saints*?
What are the Authorized Mormon Scriptures?
What are the Mormon Buildings?
What is the Mormon Eschatology?

## II. CHARACTERISTICS ..................... 27-30

Outer Characteristics
Inner Symptoms

## III. CAUSES ............................... 31-35

Causes of Growth
Root Cause of Attraction

## IV. STEPS TO SOLUTION ................. 37-75

Key Verses to Memorize
Key Passage to Read and Reread
Know the Mathematical Formula for Cults
Know the Doctrinal Test for Orthodox Christianity
Know the Answers for Major Mormon Arguments
Use the Book of Mormon to Point Out Conflicts with
   Their Own Teachings
Salvation Prayer
Know the Do's and Don'ts for Witnessing to a Mormon

## SELECTED BIBLIOGRAPHY ............ 76-77

## GRAPHICS ................................. 78-84

Mormons at Your Door
Time Line

## SCRIPTURES TO MEMORIZE ........... 85-87

# GOD'S HEART ON
# MORMONISM

## A DIFFERENT GOSPEL—A DIFFERENT GOD

Wholesome and hardworking, serious and sacrificial . . . the image of the people called Mormons is exemplary. Their personal discipline is praiseworthy. Their advertising is first class. Their business presence is booming. Their humanitarian projects get headlines. Their tithing commitment is commendable. Their young missionaries are meritorious. Men and women between ages 19 and 25 sacrifice two years of their lives as missionary volunteers. Who are these "good and upstanding people" and what do they believe?

# DEFINITIONS

# Where Did the Name *Mormon* Come From?

- According to the founder of Mormonism, Joseph Smith, *Mormon* is the name of a man who lived as an alleged prophet in America during the early fifth century A.D.

- Joseph Smith stated that the prophet Mormon compiled and abridged the records of his people into what is known today as the *Book of Mormon.*

- The name *Mormon* is now commonly used in reference to members of more than 100 church groups that believe in the *Book of Mormon.*

# Who Are the *Latter-day Saints?*

- Joseph Smith taught that from shortly after the first century until 1830, there was no true church, therefore no true saints, with authority from God on the earth. In 1834 Joseph Smith "restored" the only "true Church."

- The group has long used the word "Mormons" in reference to themselves, but there is an increasing preference for "Latter-day Saints" or just the initials "LDS" when referring to members and the full name of the church when referring to the organization.

- The two largest groups that believe in the *Book of Mormon* are:

    —The Church of Jesus Christ of Latter-day Saints (LDS).

    Headquartered in Salt Lake City, Utah, this branch is the larger of two groups, with over 10 million members worldwide.

    —The Reorganized Church of Jesus Christ of Latter-day Saints (RLDS)

    Headquartered in Independence, Missouri, the members neither call themselves Mormons nor believe in many of the LDS practices, such as baptism for the dead and polygamy. The RLDS has shunned the use of the word "Mormon" in reference to themselves or their church. In 2001, the RLDS church officially changed its name to *The Community of Christ.*

# What are the Authorized Mormon Scriptures?

Four books called "The Standard Works" make up the canon of authorized scripture for the Mormons: the Bible, the *Book of Mormon*, *Doctrine and Covenants*, and *Pearl of Great Price*.

## 1    The Bible

QUESTION: "DO MORMONS BELIEVE IN THE BIBLE?"

ANSWER:    Yes, but conditionally. Their Eighth Article of Faith says, "We believe the Bible to be the word of God as far as it is translated correctly; we also believe the *Book of Mormon* to be the word of God."

QUESTION: "DID JOSEPH SMITH ATTEMPT TO MAKE CHANGES IN THE HOLY BIBLE?"

ANSWER:    Yes. In his "Inspired Version," now usually referred to as the Joseph Smith Translation by the Utah-based Church, Smith made wholesale changes to major blocks of text, as well as smaller changes throughout most of the Bible. Included are significant changes to the book of Revelation, whose author, the apostle John, cautioned:

           *"I warn everyone who hears the words of the prophecy of this book: If anyone adds anything to them, God will add to him the plagues described in this book. And if anyone takes words away from this book of prophecy, God will take away from him his*

*share in the tree of life and in the holy city,
which are described in this book."
(Revelation 22:18-19)*

# 2     The Book of Mormon

QUESTION: "WHO WROTE THE *BOOK OF MORMON*?"

ANSWER:     Joseph Smith. The book itself, however,
claims to be an abridged record of people
living in the Americas, compiled mostly by
Mormon, the next-to-last man in a long line
of prophets/leaders. His son, Moroni, made
a few additions after Mormon's death, then
sealed and hid the record in the hill Cumorah
in what is now upper-state New York.

Smith alleged that Moroni, now resurrected,
visited him and told him where to find the
gold plates on which the record was written.
Smith claimed that he later translated the
*Book of Mormon* "by the gift and power of
God" from the "Reformed Egyptian" hieroglyphics in which it was originally written.
(No other examples of this language have
ever been found in the Americas or anywhere in the world.)

Of his book, Smith declared: *"I told the
brethren that the Book of Mormon was the
most correct of any book on earth and the
keystone of our religion, and a man would
get nearer to God by abiding by its precepts,
than by any other book."*

Interestingly, almost 4,000 corrections have been made to date since the 1830 version in "the most correct of any book." Yet the Bible says,

*"The grass withers and the flowers fall, but the Word of our God stands forever."*
*(Isaiah 40:8)*

**QUESTION:** **"WHAT DOES THE *BOOK OF MORMON* CONTAIN?"**

**ANSWER:** The *Book of Mormon* with the subtitle *Another Testament of Jesus* is said to contain an abridged history spanning more than a thousand years, from 600 B.C. to A.D. 421.

It supposedly chronicles the migration of the prophet Lehi, his family and others, from Jerusalem to the Americas, and the subsequent history of Lehi's descendants. They were divided into two nations, taking their names from two of Lehi's sons, Nephi and Laman.

The Nephites originally were the more righteous of the two groups. The Lamanites were cursed by God for their wickedness by being given dark skin. Jesus Christ, after His resurrection, supposedly visited and taught these people, resulting in a 200-year reign of unity and peace. Eventually, however, the Nephites became so wicked that, rather than cursing them with dark skin, God used the dark-skinned Lamanites to utterly destroy them.

The *Book of Mormon* is said to also contain the doctrinal teaching of the prophet leaders of the Nephites, and of Jesus Christ during His visit to the Americas.

QUESTION: **"WHY ARE CHARGES OF PLAGIARISM BROUGHT AGAINST THE *BOOK OF MORMON*?"**

ANSWER: Charges of plagiarism continue to plague Joseph Smith because of the lengthy portions of Scripture lifted from Isaiah and Matthew, yet not credited to the KJV Bible. Shorter quotations from, or obvious allusions to, both Old and New Testament passages are also scattered throughout the *Book of Mormon* without proper credit.

Although the *Book of Mormon* was supposedly written in Reformed Egyptian hieroglyphics etched on golden plates before A.D. 400 (then allegedly found and translated in 1830 by Joseph Smith), it contains much verbatim text from the King James Bible.

When paralleling the Bible, the *Book of Mormon* even contains the italicized words added in 1611 by the King James translators and not found in the underlying Greek and Hebrew manuscripts. Approximately 27,000 words from the KJV are found in *The Book of Mormon*—400 verses and portions of verses. Also, many concepts appear to be borrowed from an 1823 publication by Ethan Smith, *View of the Hebrews.*

QUESTION: "HAVE ARCHAEOLOGISTS DISCOVERED
ANY FINDINGS OF THE EARLY MORMONS'
HISTORY?"

ANSWER: No, archaeologists cannot substantiate their
reported existence. The *Book of Mormon*
describes wheeled vehicles, steel, glass,
elephants, horses and coins. According to
archaeologists, none of these existed in the
Americas during The *Book of Mormon*
time period (about 600 B.C. to A.D. 421).
The Smithsonian Institute Department of
Anthropology issued this statement:
"Smithsonian archaeologists see no con-
nection between the archaeology of the
New World (America) and the subject matter of the book [*Book of Mormon*]."

## 3     Doctrines and Covenants

QUESTION: "DOES ALL MORMON DOCTRINE COME FROM
THE BIBLE?"

ANSWER: No. The main source of doctrine is the
*Doctrine and Covenants,* first published in
1835 as a major revision of the 1833 *Book
of Commandments.*

The *Doctrine and Covenants* contains a
collection of Joseph Smith's "revelations,"
a few other significant items and most of
the doctrines distinctive to the Mormon

Church. Included would be the organization of the Church, baptism for the dead, plural celestial marriage, the three degrees of glory, the plurality of gods, and the potential of human beings becoming gods.

The Mormon doctrine that God the Father was once a mortal man living on another planet is not taught explicitly in the Mormon Standard Works. It is upheld, however, by hundreds of statements by Joseph Smith and subsequent Mormon prophets and apostles, books they have authored, and lesson manuals and other publications produced by the Mormon Church.

Occasional contradictions are difficult to explain, such as the commandment from God to Joseph Smith's wife Emma to accept his other wives (Section 132). However, the *Book of Mormon* teaches: "Behold, David and Solomon truly had many wives and concubines, which thing was abominable before me, saith the Lord" (Jacob 2:24). Since its initial publication, there have been over 65,000 changes.

# 4   Pearl of Great Price

**QUESTION:** "ARE THERE LITERARY PROBLEMS WITHIN *PEARL OF GREAT PRICE?*"

**ANSWER:** Yes. *Pearl of Great Price*, the shortest of the four standard works, contains:

— The Book of Moses: a revision of the first six chapters of Genesis.

— The Book of Abraham: alleged by Smith to be a translation of material written by Abraham on papyri. The papyri from which Smith worked have been rediscovered and shown to contain nothing but very common, very pagan, Egyptian funeral documents.

— Other writings of Joseph Smith: his revision of Matthew 23:39–24:51, autobiographical material and the thirteen Articles of Faith.

# What are the Mormon Buildings?

Most people assume that Mormon buildings have open access policies similar to those of Christian churches. However, this is untrue. Understanding the differences is important.

- **Temples**

  The Mormon temple is not a place of worship but a place where ordinances and ceremonies are administrated for both the living and the dead.

  Temple ceremonies are off limits to non-members and even to Mormons who have never reached the high level of commitment and works required for entrance. They can be entered only by those who have paid their tithes and have a "recommend" from their bishop and stake president.

  It is in the Temple that Mormons gain secret knowledge and perform the occult rituals intended to bridge the chasm from human finiteness to eventual godhood. Ezra Taft Bensen, a Mormon seer and prophet said, "Temples are the gateway to heaven . . . a bridge to the eternities."

# Temple Ceremonies

## *Washing and Anointing*

Parts of the body are ceremonially cleansed with water and anointed with oil by a temple worker so that the body can function as God intended. For example, legs are "washed" and "anointed" so they can "run and not be weary, walk and not faint."

## *Endowment*

In this special session Mormons receive instruction about their origin, purpose and eternal destiny. Temple workers give the new "patrons" secret signs and tokens which must be presented to gain entrance into the presence of God in the Celestial Kingdom. Patrons receive special undergarments to wear for the rest of their lives as a safeguard against "the power of the Destroyer" to ward off disease and bodily harm. Each patron is also assigned a new name to be used at the resurrection and in heaven.

## *Baptism for the Dead*

Worthy Mormons are allowed to repeat the baptism ceremony to help obtain salvation for non-Mormons who have died. In pursuit of this practice the Mormon Church has compiled the most extensive genealogical records in the world.

## Sealing

An ordinance performed in the authority of the Mormon priesthood by which family relationships or other blessings are promised to endure throughout eternity and not for time only. This sealing power is exercised primarily for marriage covenants and sealing children to parents, ordinances being performed for both the living and the dead. Ultimate salvation, or exaltation, is contingent upon the family unit being sealed for time and all eternity.

- **Tabernacles**

  Very few tabernacles exist. The most famous is on Temple Square in Salt Lake City, Utah, in which the famous Mormon Tabernacle Choir performs regularly. A tabernacle is like a public meeting house and is open to the general public.

- **Ward Chapels**

  The equivalent of a church, a ward chapel is a meeting place. Serving geographical territories called "wards," each building is usually equipped with a chapel, a social hall used for dances and other functions, and offices for the local leader called a Bishop. Many ward chapels are now called "churches" and serve multiple congregations.

# What is the Mormon Eschatology?

Mormon doctrine differs greatly from Biblical doctrine. Mormon theology has a man-centered doctrine that includes a pre-mortal existence in a spirit world and culminates in a heaven composed of three kingdoms. They believe in a type of "universal salvation" in which virtually all humanity will be saved, but in varying degrees of glory in the three different kingdoms. However, the Bible teaches that not all people will be saved, but that some will enter into everlasting life in heaven, and others will enter into everlasting punishment in hell.

*"They [the unrighteous]*
*will go away to eternal punishment,*
*but the righteous to eternal life."*
*(Matthew 25:46)*

- **Telestial Kingdom**

  The lowest heaven is reserved for the heathen and the wicked who reject the gospel.

- **Terrestrial Kingdom**

  The second heaven will be reserved for Christians who do not accept the Mormon message, Mormons who do not live up to their church requirements, and any other men of "good will" in other religions who live honorable lives.

- **Celestial Kingdom**

  This final heaven is also divided into three parts, in which only persons who have been sealed by celestial marriage in a Mormon temple (in person while living on earth, or later by proxy) will slowly progress toward becoming a god. At the highest level, EXAL-TATION, a man becomes a god, and he will rule with his family and populate, through procreation, a separate planet of his own.

**"WHAT DOES THE BIBLE TEACH ABOUT MEN IN THEIR EXALTED STATE BECOMING GODS?"**

The Bible teaches that there is only one true God.

*"This is what the LORD says—Israel's King and Redeemer, the LORD Almighty: I am the first and I am the last; apart from Me there is no God." (Isaiah 44:6)*

# CHARACTERISTICS

In most communities, Mormon families are highly respected and very involved in community projects. Their excellent advertising campaigns, at a yearly cost of millions of dollars, project warmth and family values. For this reason it is hard for many people to realize that the Mormon Church is not a "Christian church." Yet the apostle Paul cautioned all true Christians to be discerning:

*"I am afraid that just as Eve was deceived by the serpent's cunning, your minds may somehow be led astray from your sincere and pure devotion to Christ. For if someone comes to you and preaches a Jesus other than the Jesus we preached, or if you receive a different spirit from the one you received, or a different gospel from the one you accepted, you put up with it easily enough. For such men are false apostles, deceitful workmen, masquerading as apostles of Christ. And no wonder, for Satan himself masquerades as an angel of light. It is not surprising, then, if his servants masquerade as servants of righteousness. Their end will be what their actions deserve."*
*(2 Corinthians 11:3-4; 13-15)*

# Outer Characteristics

Mormons often look like Christians in that many have:

- Family-oriented lifestyles

- Dedication to spiritual growth

- Discipline with the prohibition of tobacco, alcohol and drugs

- Commitment to abstinence from premarital sex

- Commitment to tithing

- Emphasis on evangelism

- Appearance of being morally "perfect"

# Inner Symptoms

The zeal for "good works" that characterizes the Mormon's behavior is rooted in a belief system that says, *Performance as well as grace is prerequisite for salvation in the presence of God.* They do not know that in Jesus Christ they have been set free from the law.

*"Clearly no one is justified before God by the law,
because, 'The righteous will live by faith.'. . .
Christ redeemed us from the curse of the law
by becoming a curse for us, for it is written:
'Cursed is everyone who is hung on a tree.'"
(Galatians 3:11, 13)*

With a continual emphasis on personal achievement, many Mormons struggle with:

- **Anger** over internal discrimination
  *(Example: Temple admittance requirements too high for most Mormons)*

- **Anxiety** over life's unexpected circumstances
  *(Example: Infertile couples who are unable to provide physical bodies for spirit babies cannot meet the requirements for advancing to a higher level in heaven.)*

- **Compulsiveness** with rules and regulations
  *(Example: Compelled to do more and more in order to be "worthy")*

- **Depression** when failure occurs
  *(Example: Not advancing in the "eternal progression")*

- **Fear** of not measuring up
  *(Example: Many females fear that their husbands [or another man] might not call their secret names to enter celestial exaltation in heaven.)*

- **Guilt** from inevitable failure
  *(Example: Unable to overcome habitual "besetting sins" or otherwise meet Church standards)*

- **Low Self-Worth** when comparing self to others
  *(Example: Not keeping up with all the "callings" given by the Church superior)*

- **Pride** in good works
  *(Example: Performing multiple baptisms for the dead)*

# CAUSES

# Causes of Growth

Mormonism is growing rapidly because the church is sending approximately 60,000 full-time missionaries to spread the Mormon "gospel" around the world. Clean-cut, young missionaries dedicate two years of their lives to further their religion. Their zeal is appealing to many who are looking for truth. But the Bible exerts this caution for those who are seeking God:

*"I can testify about them*
*that they are zealous for God,*
*but their zeal is not based on knowledge."*
*(Romans 10:2)*

### "WHY ARE PEOPLE, EVEN CHRISTIANS, ATTRACTED TO THE MORMON RELIGION?"

People are attracted to Mormonism for the very reasons that people are attracted to any cult: they appeal to our three God-given inner needs for love, for significance and for security.

- Mormons appeal to our God-given need for security, our need to belong and feel accepted. The door-to-door evangelism done by wholesome-looking young missionaries and the persistent follow-up by members of a local church can give a lonely person a sense of being noticed and cared for and a feeling of being wanted.

- Mormons appeal to our God-given need for significance as they present their version of meaning and purpose in life. Their plan of salvation teaches that "you can be a god" if you learn to obey the requirements of Mormonism.

# Root Cause of Attraction

**WRONG BELIEF FOR MALES—**

"I can attain the exalted state of being a god myself if I only work hard enough." *(A way to fulfill the need for significance)*

**Biblical Truth:** The fall of man into sin occurred when Adam yielded to the temptation to try to "be like God."

*"For God knows that when you eat of it your eyes will be opened, and you will be like God, knowing good and evil." (Genesis 3:5)*

**RIGHT BELIEF FOR MALES—**

"I know from the Bible that eternal life cannot be earned or deserved based on my works. It is a free gift of God. Salvation comes by putting my faith in the Lord Jesus Christ alone."

*"For it is by grace you have been saved, through faith—and this not from yourselves, it is the gift of God—not by works, so that no one can boast." (Ephesians 2:8-9)*

**WRONG BELIEF FOR FEMALES—**

"My security comes through being married and producing children for a dedicated Mormon man who will one day call me from the grave to rule alongside him in heaven. If he (or some other man) doesn't call me by my secret name, I will stay in the grave."

***Biblical Truth:*** Spiritually, there is no distinction made between males and females. All true Christians are called "sons of God."

*"You are all sons of God through faith in Christ Jesus." (Galatians 3:26)*

**RIGHT BELIEF FOR FEMALES—**

"My security is not in my husband or any other man but in coming into a personal relationship with Jesus Christ by placing my total faith in Him and letting Him be Lord of my life."

*"There is neither Jew nor Greek,*
*slave nor free, male nor female,*
*for you are all one in Christ Jesus."*
*(Galatians 3:28)*

# STEPS TO SOLUTION

Two of the distinguishing doctrines of Latter-day Saints are polytheism—that there are many gods—and the teaching that worthy Mormons can become gods and goddesses. Knowing the following Bible verses is paramount.

# Key Verses to Memorize

*"Before Me no god was formed,*
*nor will there be one after Me.*
*I, even I, am the LORD,*
*and apart from Me there is no savior."*
*(Isaiah 43:10-11)*

# Key Passage
# to Read and Reread

Just as the apostle Paul felt great passion that all Israel be saved; today many feel that same passion that all Mormons be saved. The tenth chapter of Romans was written about those of the Jewish faith, but could easily be applied to those of the Mormon faith.

# Romans 10:1-15

Mormons have a zeal for God, but it is
not based on Biblical knowledge. ........................ *v. 2*

Instead of adhering to and receiving the
righteousness that comes from God, they
have established their own system of
righteousness. ................................................. *v. 3*

Since Christ's death fulfilled the law,
all people (including Mormons) have the
opportunity to become righteous by en-
trusting their lives to Him. ................................. *v. 4*

Moses describes "righteousness by the law"
this way: the man (Mormon) who does
righteous acts is living by his own
righteousness. ................................................. *v. 5*

"Righteous by faith" says that no amount
of human effort could have brought Jesus
down from heaven to earth or could have
raised Him from the dead. ............................... *vv. 6-7*

So what does this faith say to the Mormons? Faith says righteousness is found
in a person's heart and in the verbal ex-
pression of that faith. ....................................... *v. 8*

Mormons will be saved if they verbally
confess that Jesus is their Lord and
believe in their hearts that God raised
Him from the dead. ......................................... *v. 9*

With their hearts, Mormons can believe
and be justified, and with their mouths,
they can confess and be saved. ........................... *v. 10*

Mormons who put their trust in Jesus
will never be put to shame. ................................. *v. 11*

There is no difference between any
group of people—the same Lord is Lord
of all, and He will richly bless all who
call on Him. ....................................................... *v. 12*

Mormons who call on the name of the Lord
will be saved. ..................................................... *v. 13*

How can Mormons call on the Biblical
Jesus in whom they have not believed?
And how can they believe in this Jesus of
whom they have not heard? And how can
they hear without someone presenting the
Jesus of the Bible to them? ................................. *v. 14*

How can these presenters share the truth
unless they are sent? As it is written, "How
beautiful are the feet of those who bring
good news"—especially to the Mormons! .......... *v. 15*

# Know the Mathematical Formula for Cults

Many people wonder, "What is a cult?" A cult is a religion regarded as unorthodox or spurious. Likewise, many people wonder, "Is Mormonism a cult?" The simple answer is yes, it is a major cult today. But what kind of test could be applied to prove that it is a cult?

## The Mathematical Test for Cults

+ Does it *add* to GOD'S WORD?

− Does it *subtract* from the PERSON OF CHRIST?

X Does it *multiply* SALVATION REQUIREMENTS?

÷ Does it *divide* THE FOLLOWER'S LOYALTY?

## The Mathematical Test for *Mormonism*

### + Does it *add* to the Bible?

MORMON CLAIM:

> Apart from the Bible, there are three other revelations from God: *The Book of Mormon, Doctrine and Covenants*, and *Pearl of Great Price*.

BIBLICAL CORRECTION:

> Before Christ, God's revelation of Himself through the prophets was fragmentary, in bits and pieces as it were, *"precept upon precept; line upon line, line upon line; here a little and there a little"* (Isaiah 28:10, KJV).

In Christ, however, we have been given a full revelation of God and how to have a right relationship with Him. (See Hebrews 1:1-3; 2 Peter 1:3-4; 1 Peter 1:3-5.) There is therefore no need for, or reason to expect, any additional scriptures.

*"In the past God spoke to our forefathers through the prophets at many times and in various ways, but in these last days He has spoken to us by His Son, whom He appointed heir of all things, and through whom He made the universe. The Son is the radiance of God's glory and the exact representation of His being, sustaining all things by His powerful word. After He had provided purification for sins, He sat down at the right hand of the Majesty in heaven." (Hebrews 1:1-3)*

## — Does it *subtract* from the person of Christ?

MORMON CLAIM:

"Jesus was not the only begotten son of God in the spirit, but along with his 'brother' Lucifer, was one of innumerable spirit sons of God."

Brigham Young, the second Mormon Prophet, even taught that Adam was the father of Jesus—a doctrine the Mormon Church later rejected. "When the Virgin

Mary conceived the child Jesus, the Father had begotten him in his own likeness. He was not begotten by the Holy Ghost. And who is the Father? He is the first of the human family . . . Jesus, our elder brother, was begotten in the flesh by the same character that was in the Garden of Eden, and who is our Father in Heaven." (Brigham Young, *Journal of Discourses*, Vol. 1, p. 50-51).

## BIBLICAL CORRECTION:

Jesus is the *only* begotten Son of God. Believers *become* sons of God by faith in Christ through *adoption*

> *"For God so loved the world*
> *that He gave His one and only Son,*
> *that whoever believes in Him shall not perish*
> *but have eternal life."*
> *(John 3:16)*

# X  Does it *multiply* salvation requirements?

> "For we labor diligently to unite, to persuade our own children, and also our brethren, to believe in Christ, and to be reconciled to God, for we know that it is by grace that we are saved after all we can do" (2 Nephi 25:23, the *Book of Mormon).*

> "There is not a man or woman, who violates the covenants made with their God, that will not be required to pay the debt. The blood of Christ will never wipe that out, your own blood must atone for it" (*Journal of Discourses*, Vol. 3, p. 247). Utah is the only state in the Union that allows death by firing squad, and this is so that the condemned has the right to shed his/her blood in atonement for the sin committed. *(*Compare with *1 John 1:7.)*

**BIBLICAL CORRECTION:**

We are not to work to be saved, but are saved by grace; then out of love, works follow.

*"For it is by grace you have been saved, through faith—and this not from yourselves, it is the gift of God—not by works, so that no one can boast." (Ephesians 2:8-9)*

**"HOW DOES A PERSON RECEIVE FULL SALVATION IN MORMONISM VERSUS CHRISTIANITY?"**

In Mormonism, three requirements are essential: obedience to the laws and ordinances of the Mormon gospel, being baptized into an LDS church, and being married in a temple. In Biblical Christianity, however, salvation is gained by believing in the Lord Jesus Christ, which means receiving Him as your only Lord and Savior and giving Him control of your life. To believe means *"to rely on, to trust in"* the Lord Jesus Christ alone for salvation, not in a system of works.

*"He then brought them out and asked, 'Sirs, what must I do to be saved?' They replied, 'Believe in the Lord Jesus, and you will be saved—you and your household.'"* (Acts 16:30-31)

## ÷ Does it *divide* the follower's loyalty?

**MORMON CLAIM:**

Because the Mormon Church is supposedly the "only true church," you cannot be loyal to God without being loyal to Mormonism and its Priesthood which hold the "keys to the kingdom." In effect, this creates another mediator between God and man.

**BIBLICAL CORRECTION:**

Salvation is dependent on no one but Jesus Christ Himself who is the only mediator between God and man.

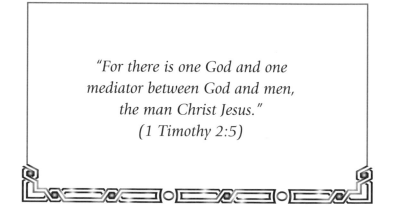

*"For there is one God and one mediator between God and men, the man Christ Jesus."*
*(1 Timothy 2:5)*

The preceding material was adapted from the Mathematical Formula of Watchman Fellowship.

# Know the Doctrinal Test for Orthodox Christianity

Every cult varies from the cardinal doctrines of the faith. Learn how Mormonism varies from five of the six essential beliefs of orthodox Christianity.

## *Virgin Birth—*

**MORMON CLAIM:**

> Jesus was not born of a virgin. Christ was the product of a physical sexual union between the Mormon God, Elohim (a resurrected man) and Mary. "[Jesus Christ] was not begotten by the Holy Ghost." (Brigham Young, *Journal of Discourses*, Vol. 1, p. 50)

**BIBLICAL CORRECTION:**

> Jesus was conceived through the Holy Spirit and born to a virgin.

> *"This is how the birth of Jesus Christ came about: His mother Mary was pledged to be married to Joseph, but before they came together, she was found to be with child through the Holy Spirit." (Matthew 1:18 )*

# *A*tonement—

Christ's agony in the Garden of Gethsemane rather than His death on the cross is the focus of atonement in Mormonism. That atonement (in Gethsemane) is necessary for full salvation but not sufficient. Mormons' own good works must be added to Christ's atonement to obtain full salvation.

**BIBLICAL CORRECTION:**

Salvation is dependent on no one but Christ Himself.

*"Salvation is found in no one else, for there is no other name under heaven given to men by which we must be saved." (Acts 4:12) (See also Ephesians 2:8-10 and John 1:12.)*

# *R*esurrection—

**MORMON CLAIM:**

Jesus rose from the dead and has a physical body of flesh and bones (the same as Christian doctrine).

**BIBLICAL CORRECTION:**

None needed.

# *Incarnation—*

Jesus was not unique in His humanity or His deity. Jesus was only one of many spirit sons of God, as was His spirit-brother Lucifer. (Milton Hunter, *Gospel Through the Ages*, page 15.)

**BIBLICAL CORRECTION:**

God became man in the unique Person of Jesus of Nazareth.

*"The Word became flesh and made His dwelling among us. We have seen His glory, the glory of the One and Only, who came from the Father, full of grace and truth."* *(John 1:14)*

# *Eschatology—*

Hell is not a place of unending punishment for anyone. Virtually everyone will eventually go to one of the three heavenly levels: the Celestial kingdom, the Terrestrial kingdom or the Telestial kingdom. (*Mormon Doctrine*, page 670.)

**BIBLICAL CORRECTION:**

An eternal hell exists for the wicked—for unbelievers whose names are not written in the Lamb's Book of Life. According to Jesus, most people will not benefit from His atoning sacrifice and receive eternal life. Instead, most will go the way of destruction.

*"If anyone's name was not found written in the book of life, he was thrown into the lake of fire." (Revelation 20:15)*

*(Also read Matthew 7:13-14 and Matthew 13:50.)*

# Scripture—

The Holy Bible is insufficient revelation from God. Three other revelations from God also exist: the *Book of Mormon*, *Doctrine and Covenants* and the *Pearl of Great Price*. If the Bible and the *Book of Mormon* differ on any topic, the *Book of Mormon's* teaching takes precedence. "We also believe the *Book of Mormon* to be the word of God" (*Articles of Faith*, Number Eight).

## BIBLICAL CORRECTION:

We are not to add to Scripture.

*"I warn everyone who hears the words of the prophecy of this book: If anyone adds anything to them, God will add to him the plagues described in this book." (Revelation 22:18)*

The Bible is God-breathed and the sole authority on spiritual matters.

*"All Scripture is God-breathed and is useful for teaching, rebuking, correcting and training in righteousness." (2 Timothy 3:16)*

# Know the Answers for Major Mormon Arguments

ARGUMENT:

MORMONISM MUST BE TRUTHFUL BECAUSE IT WAS
FOUNDED ON DIRECT REVELATIONS FROM GOD.

ANSWER:

Mormonism does claim divine inspiration. God
the Father and Jesus Christ allegedly appeared
in a vision to Joseph Smith in 1820. They told
him that all of the existing Christian churches
were in apostasy and that he would be given
the truth for a new revelation of authentic
Christianity.

Then in 1823, an angel allegedly appeared to
Smith and told him the location of certain gold
plates. Through Smith's "divinely assisted"
translation, the writings on these gold plates
became the *Book of Mormon*. Smith also had
many more alleged divine revelations in the
years that followed.

Though many people claim to receive revelations from God, this does not mean they are
God's revelations. The apostle John warned:

*"Many false prophets have gone out into the
world. This is how you can recognize the Spirit
of God: Every spirit that acknowledges that
Jesus Christ has come in the flesh is from God,
but every spirit that does not acknowledge
Jesus is not from God. . . . We are from God,
and whoever knows God listens to us; but whoever is not from God does not listen to us. This
is how we recognize the Spirit of truth and the
spirit of falsehood." (1 John 4:1-3, 6)*

In this passage, John gives two criteria for recognizing the Spirit of God and the Spirit of Truth:

— Whoever acknowledges that Jesus Christ has come in the flesh

— Whoever listens to the apostles

## • Who is Jesus Christ?

— The Alpha and the Omega, the First and the Last

— The Beginning and the End

> *"I am the Alpha and the Omega, the First and the Last, the Beginning and the End." (Revelation 22:13)*

## • Who is referred to in Isaiah 44:6?

> *"This is what the LORD says— Israel's King and Redeemer, the LORD Almighty: I am the first and I am the last; apart from Me there is no God." (Isaiah 44:6)*

— The LORD (Jehovah)—the First and Last

— God (Elohim)—the only God

> *"Acknowledge and take to heart this day that the LORD is God in heaven above and on the earth below. There is no other." (Deuteronomy 4:39)*

— The only God in heaven and on the earth

## • Who is the First and the Last?

— Jesus Christ

- **Where did Jesus Christ come from?**

  —Heaven and earth

  > *"You were shown these things so that you might know that the LORD is God; besides Him there is no other. From heaven He made you hear His voice to discipline you. On earth He showed you His great fire, and you heard His words from out of the fire." (Deuteronomy 4:35-36)*

- **How long did Jesus Christ exist before coming in the flesh?**

  —Always

  > *"Before the mountains were born or You brought forth the earth and the world, from everlasting to everlasting You are God." (Psalm 90:2)*

- **What does it mean to acknowledge that Jesus Christ has come in the flesh?**

  —It means to *agree* that Elohim—Jehovah God of the Old Testament—came to earth in human form in the person of Jesus Christ. Jesus is the Alpha and Omega—the First and the Last—the Beginning and the End—the *only* God in heaven and on earth—the Everlasting One.

- **What did the apostles teach about Jesus?**

  —Jesus is God and Savior.

  > *"To those who through the righteousness of our God and Savior Jesus Christ have received a faith as precious as ours."* (2 Peter 1:1)

  —Jesus is Lord.

  > *"My brothers, as believers in our glorious Lord Jesus Christ . . . ."* (James 2:1)

- **What does Mormonism teach about Jesus?**

  —Jehovah is the First and the Last.

  —Jesus is neither the first nor the last God, nor the one and only God for this world.

  —Jesus is a separate God from the Father and Holy Spirit and has no right to say He is Elohim.

  —Jesus has not always been God but was once spirit matter incorporated into a spirit body through the procreation process engaged in by God the Father and one of His wives, to form the spirit baby that finally progressed to Godhead.

- **What could cause such discrepancy in the two teachings?**

  The apostle Paul warned about false apostles by pointing out that *"Satan himself masquerades as an angel of light"* (2 Corinthians 11:14). Our world has false prophets, false apostles and an angelic realm that can and will deceive people into thinking they are God's messengers. Therefore, claims of divine revelation do not insure divine origin. Paul stated with certainty:

  *"Even if . . . an angel from heaven should preach a gospel other than the one we preached to you, let him be eternally condemned!" (Galatians 1:8)*

ARGUMENT:

MORMONISM AND BIBLICAL CHRISTIANITY HAVE THE SAME JESUS.

ANSWER:

This is not true. For example, Mormon doctrine denies that:

- **Jesus is born of a virgin.**

  Mormons refute that Jesus was born to a virgin. Rather, they present that Christ's physical body was the product of a physical sex act between the Heavenly Father and Mary (who in the pre-mortal existence was His own spirit daughter). Brigham Young wrote, "The birth of the Savior was as natural as the births of our children; it was the result of natural action. He partook of flesh and blood—was begotten of His Father, as we were of our fathers." (*Journal of Discourses,* 8:115) However, the Bible teaches that Jesus was conceived of the Holy Spirit.

*"What is conceived in her is from the Holy Spirit." (Matthew 1:20)*

- **Christ's deity is unique.**

  Mormon doctrine teaches that not only are there other gods before both Jesus and His Father, but also all humanity was with God "in the beginning" (*Doctrine and Covenants* 93:29).

  All people are spiritually begotten sons and daughters of God (*Journal of Discourses,* 76:24) as was Jesus a son, and all people are eternal beings with the potential of likewise progressing to Godhood (Ibid., 76:58; 132:19-20).

  Mormon leaders and church lesson manuals frequently refer to Christ as "the Only Begotten *in the flesh.*" However, the Bible teaches that He is the only begotten Son of God, period. There is no textual support in any ancient, Biblical manuscript for adding "in the flesh."

  *"For God so loved the world that He gave His one and only Son, that whoever believes in Him shall not perish but have eternal life." (John 3:16)*

- **Christ's existence with the Father was unique.**

  Nowhere in the Bible is any other man said to have been with God in the beginning, much less that *he was God* in the beginning.

  *"In the beginning was the Word [Christ], and the Word was with God, and the Word was God." (John 1:1)*

- **Christ created everyone and everything on earth.**

  All people and things on earth were created by Him.

  *"Through Him [Christ] all things were made; without Him nothing was made that has been made." (John 1:3)*

- **Christ created everything in heaven.**

  Nothing existed eternally, but all things came into being.

  *"For by Him all things were created: things in heaven and on earth, visible and invisible, whether thrones or powers or rulers or authorities; all things were created by Him and for Him." (Colossians 1:16)*

### JESUS HAD MULTIPLE WIVES.

#### *Teaching:*

Mormon leaders have taught in General Conferences that Jesus was married at Cana of Galilee to Lazarus' sisters, Mary and Martha, as well as to Mary Magdalene.

#### ANSWER:

Nowhere does the Bible mention any marriage or any wives of Jesus. But more importantly, Jesus considered polygamy and sexual relations outside of a monogamous marriage to be sin. Jesus taught that any man who divorced his wife, for any cause other than fornication, and married another woman would be committing adultery.

*"I tell you that anyone who divorces his wife, except for marital unfaithfulness, and marries another woman commits adultery." (Matthew 19:9)*

The Jesus of the Bible was sinless and therefore never entered into polygamous marriages.

*"God made Him who had no sin to be sin for us, so that in Him we might become the righteousness of God." (2 Corinthians 5:21)*

### JESUS HAD CHILDREN BY HIS WIVES.

*Teaching:*

> Mormon leaders say that Jesus had children, whose descendants are still on the earth.

ANSWER:

> This Mormon teaching runs counter to the following Messianic prophecy which conservative theologians traditionally say refers to Christ.
>
> *"By oppression and judgment He was taken away. And who can speak of His descendants? For He was cut off from the land of the living; for the transgression of my people He was stricken." (Isaiah 53:8)*
>
> This passage clearly indicates that Jesus would have no earthly children. However, when Isaiah 53:10 in the King James Version says the Messiah *"shall see His seed,"* the context indicates, and scholars agree, that the seed spoken of here are born-again believers, adopted sons and daughters of God through Jesus Christ (Romans 8:15-16; Galatians 4:5-6; Ephesians 1:5). Though the Mormon apostle attempted to use Isaiah 53:10 to bolster the claim that Jesus had natural children, the Book of Mormon itself contradicts that idea in Mosiah 15:10-13.

**JESUS ATONED FOR SIN WHEN HE SWEATED BLOOD IN THE GARDEN OF GETHSEMANE.**

### Teaching:

The Mormon Jesus made Atonement for sin, not so much by His death on the Cross as by His suffering in the Garden of Gethsemane. This is supposed to have been accomplished by His suffering so deeply that he sweat blood.

*"Behold, blood cometh from every pore, so great shall be his anguish for the wickedness and the abominations of his people."* (Book of Mormon, Mosiah 3:7)

### ANSWER:

While Mormonism links the atonement to the Cross in a relatively minor way, the primary emphasis is on Gethsemane as the place where the suffering of Jesus made possible the forgiveness of sins. The primary "proof-text" from the Bible used by Mormons to support the garden atonement doctrine is Luke 22:44.

However, this passage neither says that Jesus sweat great drops of blood from every pore of His body—nor indicates that He sweat blood at all. The phrase "as it were" in King James English is the equivalent of "like" in modern English. It is a form of expression that is called a simile, comparing one thing to another as being similar.

*"Being in an agony He prayed more earnestly: and His sweat was as it were great drops of blood falling down to the ground." (Luke 22:44, KJV)*

Mormonism teaches that Jesus' redemptive work on the cross, and thus the shedding of His blood there, His death, is not sufficient for man's complete salvation. To Christ's work must be added the works and personal righteousness of the Mormon "gods in embryo." Both Christ's work and their own works are essential prerequisites to receiving full salvation—Godhood. Quite unlike this, the Jesus of Biblical Christianity saves individuals apart from their own works or law keeping.

*"Now when a man works, his wages are not credited to him as a gift, but as an obligation. However, to the man who does not work but trusts God who justifies the wicked, his faith is credited as righteousness. David says the same thing when he speaks of the blessedness of the man to whom God credits righteousness apart from works." (Romans 4:4-6)*

Clearly there are great differences between the Mormon Jesus and the Jesus of the Bible. Mormonism presents its unbiblical doctrines about Christ as "additional" information. Unfortunately. it is not merely additional and unbiblical, it is anti-biblical, anti-Christian, contrary information that cannot be reconciled with the Bible's teaching on Christ.

The Biblical Jesus:

- was born of a virgin (Matthew 1:18, 20)

- was uniquely God (John 1:18)

- was uniquely sinless (2 Corinthians 5:21; Hebrews 4:15).


By the sacrifice of His perfect life, His death on the Cross, alone, Jesus atoned for the sins of His people, who receive Him by faith and are born of God (John 1:12-13; Romans 5:1; 1 Peter 1:3-5). These things are not true of the Mormon Jesus.

# Use the Book of Mormon to Point Out Conflicts with Their Own Teachings

Mormonism's own writings are rife with contradictions. Between its scriptures and its current teachings, Mormon writings are in conflict with each other. The Mormon Church cannot be relied on to believe and obey its own scriptures.

- **Mormon Teaching—**

    A Mormon can be baptized for a dead relative to make that relative's salvation possible.

    *"We have the privilege of being baptized for our dead, and performing other ordinances for them, and thus become saviors on Mount Zion."* (Charles C. Rich, *Journal of Discourses,* vol. 19, p.255). Rich was a Mormon apostle.

    **— *Conflict with Writings:***

    ***Book of Mormon—***

    *"For behold, this life is the time for men to prepare to meet God; yea, behold the day of this life is the day for men to perform their labors. And now, as I said unto you before, as ye have had so many witnesses, therefore, I beseech of you that ye do not procrastinate the day of your repentance until the end; for after this day of life, which is given us to prepare for eternity, behold, if we do not improve our time while in this life, then cometh*

*the night of darkness wherein there can be no labor performed. Ye cannot say, when ye are brought to that awful crisis, that I will repent, that I will return to my God. Nay, ye cannot say this; for that same spirit which doth possess your bodies at the time that ye go out of this life, that same spirit will have power to possess your body in that eternal world. For behold, if ye have procrastinated the day of your repentance even until death, behold, ye have become subjected to the spirit of the devil, and he doth seal you his; therefore, the Spirit of the Lord hath withdrawn from you, and hath no place in you, and the devil hath all power over you; and this is the final state of the wicked." (Alma 34:32-35)*

### Bible—

*"As it is appointed unto men once to die, but after this the judgment." (Hebrews 9:27, KJV)*

## • Mormon Teaching—

God developed from being a man on another world, and human beings can become gods and goddesses.

*"As man now is, God once was. As God now is, man may be . . . A son of God, like God to be, would not be robbing deity" (Teachings of Lorenzo Snow, p. 9).*

*— Conflict with Writings:*

### Book of Mormon —

*"For I know that god is neither a change-able being but He is unchangeable from all eternity to all eternity." (Moroni 8:18)*

### Bible—

*"Before the mountains were brought forth, or ever Thou hadst formed the earth and the world, even from everlasting to ever-lasting, Thou art God." (Psalm 90:2, KJV)*

## • Mormon Teaching—

There are many gods. (*Pearl of Great Price*—Abraham, 4:1-31; *Teachings of the Prophet Joseph Smith*, pp. 346, 370-75)

*— Conflict with Writings:*

### Book of Mormon—

*"And after this manner shall ye baptize in my name; for behold, verily I say unto you, that the Father, and the Son, and the Holy Ghost are one; and I am in the Father, and the Father in me, and the Father and I are one." (3 Nephi 11:27)*

### Bible—

*"There is one God, and one mediator between God and men, the man Christ Jesus." (1 Timothy 2:5, KJV)*

- **Mormon teaching—**

    God changes, must always progress, or else begin regression, potentially even to the point of ceasing to be God. Contradicting Mormon apostle Orson Pratt, President of Brigham Young University taught:

    ". . . Brother Orson Pratt has, in theory, bounded the capacity of God. According to his theory, God can progress no further in knowledge and power; but the God that I serve is progressing eternally . . ." (*Journal of Discourses*, 11:286).

— *Conflict with Writings:*

    ### Book of Mormon—

    *"For do we not read that God is the same yesterday, today, and forever, and in him there is no variableness neither shadow of changing? And now, if ye have imagined up unto yourselves a god who doth vary, and in whom there is shadow of changing, then have ye imagined up unto yourselves a god who is not a God of miracles. But behold, I will show unto you a God of miracles, even the God of Abraham, and the God of Isaac, and the God of Jacob; and it is the same God who created the heavens and the earth, and all things that in them are."* (Mormon 9:9-11)

*Bible—*

*"Every good gift and every perfect gift is from above, and cometh down from the Father of lights, with whom is no variableness, neither shadow of turning." (James 1:17, KJV)*

## • **Mormon Teaching—**

God the Father has a physical body as an essential part of his being (*Doctrine and Covenants* 130:22).

## — *Conflict with Writings:*

### *Book of Mormon—*

*"The king said: Is God that Great Spirit that brought our fathers out of the land of Jerusalem? And Aaron said unto him: Yea, he is that Great Spirit, and he created all things both in heaven and in earth. Believest thou this? And he said: Yea, I believe that the Great Spirit created all things, and I desire that ye should tell me concerning all these things, and I will believe thy words and man can become God." (Alma 22:9-11)*

### *Bible—*

*"God is a Spirit: and they that worship Him must worship Him in spirit and in truth." (John 4:24, KJV)*

Anyone can be sincere and yet sincerely wrong. Do you think that some of the teachings you've been taught have been in error? Do you feel led by the Lord to line up your life with the Bible?

Are you being convicted to renounce false teaching and turn to Jesus Christ alone for your salvation? He invites you to enter into a relationship with Him that will last forever. If that's the need in your heart, pray this prayer:

# *Salvation Prayer*
## *Heavenly Father,*

*I admit that I have sinned. I know I have broken Your laws, and I'm not worthy to be in Your presence. Please forgive me for all my sins.*

*I realize that Jesus Christ is the one and only Savior. I'm no longer trusting in my good works or ordinances to save me. Neither am I relying on obeying any rules or laws to save me.*

*Jesus, thank You for dying on the cross for my sins. Right now, I recognize that You rose from the dead and offer me full salvation in the presence of God as a free gift. I ask You to come into my heart to be my Lord and my Savior. Make me the person You want me to be.*

*In Your holy name, I pray. Amen*

# Know the DO's and DON'Ts for Witnessing to a Mormon

*Do:* Develop a personal relationship with the Mormon.

> *"As iron sharpens iron, so one man sharpens another." (Proverbs 27:17)*

*Don't:* Make assumptions about a Mormon, particularly about personal beliefs. Not all Mormons believe alike. When dealing with doctrine, avoid phrases like "You believe," or even "Mormons believe." Instead, refer to the Mormon Church itself or to Mormon scriptures or leaders, quoting what they have actually said, written or otherwise published.

> *"A wise man's heart guides his mouth, and his lips promote instruction." (Proverbs 16:23)*

*Do*: Be gentle and kind when confronting. At all costs, avoid rudeness, arrogance or doctrinal brutality that tries to correct immediately every error at every turn. Many errors that are not core to the discussion may be temporarily sidestepped.

> *"The Lord's servant must not quarrel; instead, he must be kind to everyone, able to teach, not resentful. Those who oppose him he must gently instruct, in the hope that God will grant them repentance leading them to a knowledge of the truth." (2 Timothy 2:24-25)*

**Don't:** Be afraid to be bold. Mormons often view bold-ness as evidence of commitment and authority.

> *"For God did not give us a spirit of timidity, but a spirit of power, of love and of self-discipline." (2 Timothy 1:7)*

**Do:** Research to become familiar with key Mormon writings, doctrines and teachings.

> *"It is not good to have zeal without knowledge, nor to be hasty and miss the way." (Proverbs 19:2)*

**Don't:** Assume that Mormons know all the teachings of their church.

> *"A fool finds no pleasure in understanding but delights in airing his own opinions." (Proverbs 18:2)*

**Do:** Ask Mormons if Jesus can save people from their sins, granting complete, permanent forgive-ness of all sins and providing eternal life in the presence of God without the mediating help of any other person or organization.

> *"Salvation is found in no one else, for there is no other name under heaven given to men by which we must be saved." (Acts 4:12)*

**Don't:** Allow yourself to be sidetracked. Obtain a clear answer to the questions above. A clear answer would be either "Yes," "No," or even "I really don't know." Don't be "conformed to this world" in thinking that exposing and refuting error is bad just because it is negative.

*"Do not conform any longer to the pattern of this world, but be transformed by the renewing of your mind. Then you will be able to test and approve what God's will is—His good, pleasing and perfect will." (Romans 12:2)*

**Do:** Find out what the Mormon believes. Ask questions like, "Why did you decide to join the Mormon Church?" or "What do you like most about the Mormon Church?" You may find that the Mormon's reasons for joining or for staying center more on relationships and family than on doctrine. This can affect how you should approach witnessing to the Mormon.

*"The heart of the discerning acquires knowledge; the ears of the wise seek it out." (Proverbs 18:15)*

**Don't:** Assume you are talking the same language— define your terms. Mormons frequently use the same terms as Christians. However, they assign different meanings to them. For example, Joseph Smith said this about God:

*"I will go back to the beginning before the world was, to show what kind of a being God is. . . . God himself was once as we are now, and is an exalted man. . . . I am going to tell you how God came to be God. We have imagined and supposed that God was God from all eternity. I will refute that idea, and take away the veil, so that you may see. . . .*

*"He was once a man like us; . . . God him-self, the Father of us all, dwelt on an earth, the same as Jesus Christ did. . . . Here, then, is eternal life—to know the only wise and true God; and you have got to learn how to be gods yourselves, and to be kings and priests to God, the same as all gods have done before you . . ."* (Joseph Smith, *History of the Church,* Vol. 6, p. 305-6).

God—Father, Son and Holy Spirit—is the only God in all existence.

*"Acknowledge and take to heart this day that the LORD is God in heaven above and on the earth below. There is no other." (Deuteronomy 4:39)*

*Do:*    Help the Mormon recognize the reliability of the **Bible.**

### — It is the Word of God.

*"All Scripture is God-breathed and is useful for teaching, rebuking, correct-ing and training in righteousness." (2 Timothy 3:16)*

— It has unity of meaning even though written over a span of 1600 years in three different languages with forty different authors.

• *It has been meticulously preserved over time because Hebrew scribes were perfec-tionists in their copying of the Scriptures.*

- *It has manuscript evidence which far exceeds that of any other ancient writing.*

The number of manuscript copies of the Scriptures surviving from antiquity down to our day far exceeds the number of manuscripts representing any other ancient writing. There exists 5,366 ancient Greek New Testament manuscripts or fragments—the closest competition would be Homer's *The Iliad*, of which only 643 ancient copies exist. Other well-known ancient writings survive in only a handful of documents. The time span between the writing date of the oldest surviving New Testament manuscript fragment and its original writing date is 50–75 years. Most other ancient writings survive in copies made anywhere from 800 to 1300 years after their original composition. No legitimate reason can be advanced for doubting both the authenticity and integrity (accurate transmission) of the New Testament.

* The statistics in the preceding paragraph were taken from *A General Introduction to the Bible,* by Norman Geisler and William Nix, pp. 385, 404-5, 475.

- *It can never be destroyed or lost.*

   *"The grass withers and the flowers fall, but the word of our God stands forever." (Isaiah 40:8)*

**Don't:** Use any paraphrasing or quote from any Bible translation except the King James Version. This is the only version that Mormons see as authoritative.

**Do:** Use your personal Christian testimony.

*"A truthful witness saves lives, but a false witness is deceitful." (Proverbs 14:25)*

**Don't:** Believe that a testimony grounded in Scripture alone is somehow inferior to a supernatural sign-based testimony. Supernatural and spiritual signs such as a "burning in the bosom" are not required either for the Spirit to lead or for the Christian to have confidence in His leading. Indeed, Jesus taught that *"An evil and adulterous generation seeketh after a sign"* (Matthew 12:39, KJV). Christians trust in the promise of the Spirit to guide them into the truth.

*"When He, the Spirit of truth, comes, He will guide you into all truth. He will not speak on His own; He will speak only what He hears, and He will tell you what is yet to come." (John 16:13)*

**Don't forget to be patient and pray.**

> *"Pray continually."*

# Selected Bibliography

• • • • • • • • • • • • • • • • • • • • • • • • • • • • •

*With grateful appreciation for editorial review by
Watchman Fellowship, Inc. www. watchman.org*

Ankerbereg, John, and John Weldon. *The Facts on the
Mormon Church.* The Anker Series. Eugene, Ore.:
Harvest House, 1991.

Brodie, Fawn M. *No Man Knows My History: The Life of
Joseph Smith, The Mormon Prophet.* 2d ed. New York:
Alfred A. Knopf, 1971.

Cares, Mark J. *Speaking the Truth in Love to Mormons,* 2d
ed. Milwaukee, WI; WELS Outreach Resources, 1998.
[Recommended]

Fraser, Gordon H. *Is Mormonism Christian?* Chicago:
Moody, 1977.

Hunter, Milton R. *The Gospel Through the Ages.* Salt Lake
City: Stephen and Wallis, 1945.

Larson, Charles M. *By His Own Hand upon Papyrus:
A New Look at the Joseph Smith Papyri,* Rev. ed.
Grand Rapids: Institute for Religious Research, 1992.
[Recommended]

Martin, Walter. *The Maze of Mormonism.* 2d ed. Ventura,
Calif.: Regal, 1978.

McConkie, Bruce R. *Mormon Doctrine.* 2d ed. Salt Lake
City: Bookcraft, 1966.

Morey, Robert A. *How to Answer a Mormon: Practical Guidelines for What to Expect and What to Reply When the Mormons Come to Your Door*. Minneapolis, Minn.: Bethany House, 1983.

Smith, Joseph Fielding. Teachings of the Prophet Joseph Smith. Salt Lake City: Deseret, 1977.

Smith, Joseph Jr. "The Articles of Faith." *In The Pearl of Great Price*. Salt Lake City: The Church of Jesus Christ of Latter-Day Saints, n.d.

Smith, Joseph Jr. *History of the Church of Jesus Christ of Latter-Day Saints*. 7 vols. Salt Lake City: Deseret, 1978.

Spencer, James R. *Have You Witnessed to a Mormon Lately?* Old Tappan, N. J.: Chosen Books, 1986.

Tanner, Jerald, and Sandra Tanner. *The Changing World of Mormonism*. Revised ed. Chicago: Moody, 1981.

Williams, Clyde J. *The Teachings of Lorenzo Snow*. Salt Lake City: Bookcraft, 1984.

Young, Brigham. *Journal of Discourses*. 26 vols. Liverpool, England: F.D. and S.W. Richards, 1954-86.

# MORMONS
## AT YOUR
# DOOR

*What You Should Do When
Mormons Come Knocking*

**REFLECT THE LOVE OF CHRIST.**

Mormons are accustomed to the blast of a slamming
door. Therefore, kind and courteous communication on
your part could open the door of their hearts to Christ.

**REALIZE THE MORMON PERSPECTIVE.**

Mormonism, like many other world religions and cults,
operates on a "works theology." Mormons are taught that
full salvation is conditional, requiring not only God's
grace but also their own obedience, performance of good
works, and adherence to the rules of the Mormon Church.
Their deep desire to earn salvation is probably the reason
they are knocking on your door. *But the Bible clearly
teaches that salvation is only by God's grace through faith
in Christ—not by works (Ephesians 2:8-9) and that grace
and works cannot be mixed (Romans 11:6).*

## RECOGNIZE DEVIANT MEANINGS.

Mormons will use the same Christian words you do, but with different meanings. *For example, "God" is not the sole being who is eternal, transcendent and all-powerful* (Isaiah 45:5) *but rather one of many deities who was once a man. "Jesus Christ" is not the only begotten Son of God* (John 3:16) *but rather one of many spirit children of Elohim (God) and his wife.* Even with Christian-sounding talk, Mormons are speaking a different language.

## REACH OUT BY ASKING QUESTIONS.

When others disagreed with Him, Jesus frequently responded by asking penetrating questions. When the Mormons are explaining their teachings to you, sensitively ask, *"If our works are necessary for earning salvation, doesn't that mean that Christ's Atonement is insufficient? Isn't this a type of self-righteousness? Wouldn't this make salvation by works rather than by grace?"*

## REFER TO YOUR BIBLE.

Use the King James Version if you have one, since that's the only version Mormons recognize. With your Bible handy, continue to ask penetrating questions about Christ, salvation and the afterlife. For example, open your Bible and ask them to read Isaiah 44:6, *"This is what the LORD says—Israel's King and Redeemer, the LORD Almighty: I am the first and I am the last; apart from Me there is no God."* Then ask, *"In light of this, how can members of your church become gods?"* Another example: *"If there are three heavens (a Mormon teaching), why does Revelation 21 speak of only one place where God will live with all believers for eternity?"*

If the Mormons seem interested, write the Biblical references on a piece of paper for them to take home. Don't let frustration make you harsh or overbearing. Remember, the outcome is in God's hands. Your goal is not simply to win an argument, but to cause the Mormons to question their own faith and become curious about yours.

### REALIZE YOU DON'T HAVE ALL THE ANSWERS.

If you don't know the answer to a question, simply say, *"I'd be happy to get that information for you if you'd like to come back and discuss it some time."* Saying this will keep the door open for future visits and also keep you from becoming defensive.

### REALIZE THAT THE TRUTH CAN HURT.

Facing the truth about Mormonism can be very painful for a "true believer" Mormon. This may result in angry outbursts. Have compassion and patience. *"A gentle answer turns away wrath"* (Proverbs 15:1). Be prepared to gently show the Mormon the importance of accepting truth, even when it hurts to do so.

### RELATE YOUR PERSONAL TESTIMONY.

Describe what a difference Jesus has made in your life. Speak from the heart. Talk about your relationship with Christ and what He means to you.

### REINFORCE TRUTH WITH TRACTS.

Many Mormons have been converted this way. They can read the tract over and over again in privacy, where the Holy Spirit can do His work.

### REMAIN ENCOURAGED.

Mormon missionaries are rarely converted while making house calls. However, the Holy Spirit can use your penetrating questions, the gospel tract and your loving spirit to work on their hearts.

### REMEMBER TO PRAY.

Pray for the visitors who have knocked on your door. God may have arranged for you to have a special encounter with those who are ready to open the door of their hearts to Christ. *"Pray continually"* (1 Thessalonians 5:17).

# TIME LINE
## The Development of the Mormon Church

| | |
|---|---|
| December 23, 1805 | Birth of Joseph Smith, Jr. in Sharon, Vermont. |
| Spring, 1820 | First vision of Joseph Smith. As an adult, Smith claims that when he was 14 years old, God the Father and Jesus Christ appeared in the "Sacred Grove," telling him that all churches were wrong and that he was later to restore the only true church. (Earlier versions of the same story contained different and contradictory accounts.) |
| September 21-23, 1823 | Second vision is the angel Moroni, the son of the prophet Mormon, telling Joseph Smith where to locate the golden plates upon which is engraved the Word of God in re-formed Egyptian hieroglyphics. |
| September 22, 1827 | Moroni grants Joseph Smith permission to translate the plates with the aid of magical glasses, which he calls Urim and Thummim. As Joseph Smith sits on one side of a tall curtain, he dictates the *Book of Mormon* to friends such as Oliver Cowdery and Martin Harris, who serve as scribes. |

| | |
|---|---|
| May 15, 1829 | Third vision of Joseph Smith is John the Baptist telling him that he and Cowdery are to baptize and ordain each other into the Aaronic priesthood. |
| April 6, 1830 | Mormonism, then called Church of Christ, is officially organized with six charter members. |
| 1831 | The Mormons move to Kirkland, Ohio. The first temple is established. |
| 1832 | The Mormons move to Independence, Missouri, to their new Jerusalem, their new "Zion," which Smith claims is the original Garden of Eden and will be the location of Christ's return and reign during the millennium. |
| 1838-39 | Joseph Smith is imprisoned in Missouri. After escaping from jail and rejoining Mormons driven from Missouri into Illinois, Smith directs Church land purchases and builds up the town of Nauvoo. |
| June 27, 1844 | Smith unveils new doctrines: Baptism for the dead and Celestial Marriage (for time and all eternity, and plural). Latter doctrine sparks controversy leading to the murder of Joseph Smith and his brother Hyrum by an angry mob in Carthage, Illinois. |

| | |
|---|---|
| 846-47 | Driven by mob violence from Nauvoo, Brigham Young leads the Mormons on a treacherous journey to the great Salt Lake in Utah, founding Salt Lake City. |
| 1890 | Mormon President Wilford Woodruff issues a Manifesto denying charges of recent plural marriages in the Church and saying his *advice to the Latter-day Saints is to refrain from contracting any marriage forbidden by the law of the land* (emphasis added). Polygamy continues covertly until 1904. |
| 1947 | The Mormon Church reaches one million in membership. |
| 1976 | Brigham Young's Adam-God doctrine is officially denounced by Mormon Prophet Spencer W. Kimball during General Conference. |
| 1978 | Mormon Prophet Spencer W. Kimball receives a new revelation allowing black men to hold the Mormon Priesthood for the first time. |
| 1982 | The Mormon Church reaches five million in membership. |
| 1997 | The Mormon Church reaches ten million in membership. |

# Biblical Answers to Mormon Teachings
## Scriptures to Memorize

● ● ● ● ● ● ● ● ● ● ● ● ● ● ● ● ● ● ● ● ● ● ● ● ● ● ● ● ● ● ● ● ● ● ● ● ●

MORMON TEACHING: GOD ONCE A MAN

*"God himself was **once as we are now** and is an exalted man. . . ."* (*Teachings of the Prophet Joseph Smith*, p. 345)

BIBLICAL ANSWER: *"Before the mountains were born or You brought forth the earth and the world, **from everlasting to everlasting You are God.**" (Psalm 90:2)*

MORMON TEACHING: JESUS NOT GOD IN THE TRINITY

*"**Christ**, the Firstborn, was the mightiest of all the **spirit children** of the Father."* (*Doctrine and Covenants*, 93:21-23)

BIBLICAL ANSWER: *"In the beginning was the Word, and the Word was with God, and the **Word was God**. . . . The Word became flesh and made His dwelling among us. We have seen His glory, the glory of the One and Only, Who came from the Father." (John 1:1,14)*

MORMON TEACHING: JESUS NOT BORN OF A VIRGIN

*"Christ was begotten by an Immortal Father [God] in the same way that mortal men are begotten by mortal fathers."* (Bruce R. McConkie, *Mormon Doctrine*, p. 547)

BIBLICAL ANSWER: *"Mary was pledged to be married to Joseph, but before they came together, she was found to be with child **through the Holy Spirit**. . . . But he had no union with her until she gave birth to a son. And he gave Him the name Jesus." (Matthew 1:18,25)*

• • • • • • • • • • • • • • • • • • • • • • • • • • • • • • • •

MORMON TEACHING: SALVATION REQUIRES WORKS

" . . . *It is by grace that we are saved, after **all we can do**."* (*Book of Mormon*, Nephi 25:23b)

BIBLICAL ANSWER: *"It is by grace you have been saved, through faith—and this not from yourselves, it is the gift of God—**not by works**, so that no one can boast." (Ephesians 2:8-9)*

MORMON TEACHING: PRE-MORTAL EXISTENCE

*"Known as Michael, the archangel in the pre-mortal existence, and Ancient of Days, Adam was the first man, and was created in the likeness of God."* (*LDS Church News*, January 3, 1998)

BIBLICAL ANSWER: *"The LORD God formed the man from the dust of the ground and breathed into his nostrils the breath of life, and the man became a living being." (Genesis 2:7)*

MORMON TEACHING: POLYTHEISM

*"You have got to learn how to be **Gods yourselves**."* (*Teachings of the Prophet Joseph Smith*, p. 346)

BIBLICAL ANSWER: *"This is what the LORD says— Israel's King and Redeemer, the LORD Almighty: I am the first and I am the last; apart from Me there is no God." (Isaiah 44:6)*

MORMON TEACHING: JESUS BORN AT JERUSALEM

*"And behold, He shall be born of Mary **at Jerusalem**."* (*Book of Mormon*, Alma 7:10a)

BIBLICAL ANSWER: *"Jesus was born* **in Bethlehem** *in Judea, during the time of King Herod."* *(Matthew 2:1)*

MORMON TEACHING: MAN EXALTED TO GOD
*"As God is,* **man may become** *. . ."* (*Articles of Faith,* p.430)

BIBLICAL ANSWER: *"Acknowledge and take to heart this day that the LORD is God in heaven above and on the earth below. There is no other."* *(Deuteronomy 4:39)*

MORMON TEACHING: CHRIST'S SACRIFICE NOT ALL SUFFICIENT
*Those who violate God's covenants. " . . . the blood of Christ will never wipe that out,* **your own blood will have to atone for it.**" (Brigham Young, *Journal of Discourses,* Vol. III, p. 247; Vol. IV, pp. 219-220)

BIBLICAL ANSWER: *"***The blood of Jesus***, His Son,* ***purifies us from all sin.***" *(1 John 1:7)*

MORMON TEACHING: ALL PEOPLE ARE BORN GOD'S CHILDREN
*"All men and women are . . . literally the sons and daughters of Deity. . . . Man as a spirit, was begotten and born of heavenly parents . . . prior to coming upon the earth."* (Gospel Principles p. 11)

BIBLICAL ANSWER: *"To all who* **received Him***, to those who believed in His name, He gave* **the right to become children of God.**" *(John 1:12)*

# ℬIBLICAL 𝒦EYS . . .

are "people helper" resources based on the fundamental truths of the Bible. **Biblical Keys** are available on approximately 100 topics.

Many of the topics complement or will "come alongside" to help you develop more insight on the subject of *Mormonism*.

## RELATED TOPICS

*Cults*

*Jehovah's Witnesses*

*New Age Spirituality*

*The Occult*

*Satan, Demons & Satanism*

*Spiritual Warfare*

*For a complete listing of topics and to request a product catalog—*
**call toll free—**

## 1-800-488-HOPE (4673).
**www.hopefortheheart.org**